SQUANTO AND
THE FIRST THANKSGIVING

First Steck-Vaughn Edition 1992

Library of Congress number: 89-3822

Library of Congress Cataloging in Publication Data.

Celsi, Teresa Noel.
  Squanto and the first Thanksgiving/Teresa Noel Celsi; illustrated by Pamela Ford Johnson.

  (Real readers)
  Summary: A simple biography of the Patuxet Indian who helped the Pilgrims survive in their early days in the Plymouth colony.
    1. Squanto—Juvenile literature. 2. Patuxet Indians—Biography—Juvenile literature. 3. Indians of North America—Massachusetts—Biography—Juvenile literature. 4. Thanksgiving Day—Juvenile literature. [1. Squanto. 2. Patuxet Indians—Biography. 3. Indians of North America—Biography. 4. Thanksgiving Day.] I. Johnson, Pamela Ford, ill. II. Title. III. Series.
  GT4975.C45   1989   970.004′97—dc19 [92]   89-3822

ISBN 0-8172-3511-6   hardcover library binding

ISBN 0-8114-6710-4   softcover binding

 3 4 5 6 7 8 9 0   96 95 94 93 92

SQUANTO
and the
First Thanksgiving

by Teresa Celsi
illustrated by Pam Ford Johnson

STECK-VAUGHN
C O M P A N Y
A Subsidiary of National Education Corporation

In 1620, the Pilgrims came to America.
They came from England to make
homes at Plymouth.

At first, the Pilgrims had a bad time at Plymouth. They did not have food to eat. They did not have homes yet. One by one, the Pilgrims fell sick.

At that time, there were American Indians at Plymouth, too. The Indians had homes in the hills.

The Indians could see the Pilgrims. But they did not know if they wanted to meet the Pilgrims. The Pilgrims looked odd to the Indians. The Indians did not know if they could be friends.

But one Indian did go to meet the Pilgrims and make friends. This Indian was named Squanto.

Squanto wanted to find out what the Pilgrims were doing at Plymouth. He went to meet the Pilgrims.

The Pilgrims were glad to meet Squanto. A Pilgrim named William Bradford said to Squanto, "We are here to make new homes. We want to be your friends. Can you help us make friends with the other Indians?"

Squanto liked the Pilgrims. He could see that they needed help. He helped the Pilgrims make friends with the other Indians. He helped the Pilgrims do other things, too.

Squanto helped the Pilgrims find fish to eat from the lake by Plymouth.

"Look," Squanto said to the Pilgrims. "Do what you see me do."

Squanto got a net. He put the net in the lake. In time, Squanto had a big fish in the net!

"See?" said Squanto. "Here is a big fish for you to eat."

Squanto helped the Pilgrims get corn to eat.

"Look," he said to the Pilgrims. "Do what you see me do."

Squanto made a little hill. He put a hole in the top. He put 1, 2, 3 seeds in the hole. He put a little fish in the hole, too.

"The little fish will help the corn get big," Squanto said.

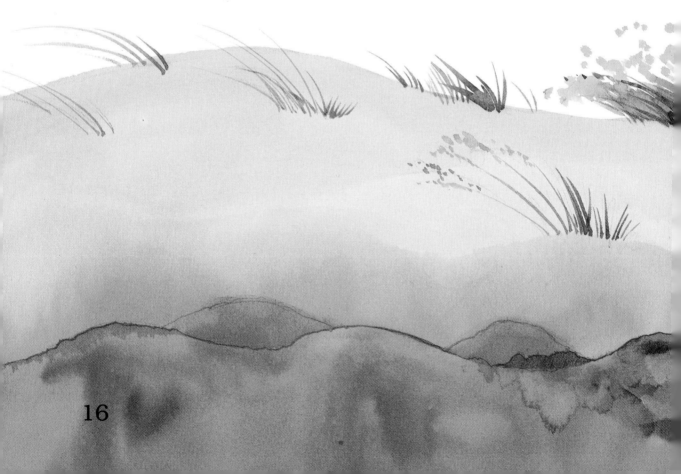

Squanto helped the sick Pilgrims get well. He helped the Pilgrims find big turkeys to eat in the hills by Plymouth. Squanto helped the Pilgrims make good homes, too.

One day, William Bradford said to Squanto, "You have helped us. We want to have a feast to give thanks for all the good things we have now. Go and tell the Indians to come to the feast."

Squanto went to the other Indians.

"Come and eat with the Pilgrims," said Squanto. "They are going to have a big feast. They want to thank us for being good friends."

The Pilgrims baked and baked. They made good things to eat. The Pilgrims went to the lake for fish and to the hills for turkeys. They all made food for the big feast.

The day for the feast came. Squanto
and the other Indians came with good
things to eat.

The Pilgrims and the Indians all sat down to eat. There was corn. There were fish from the lake. There was the food that the Indians had come with. There was good food for all!

"Now," said William Bradford, "we will give thanks. We give thanks to the Lord for this good food. We give thanks for the homes we now have. We give thanks for all the new friends we have made here.

And we give thanks to Squanto. He helped us plant the good corn and find the fish and the turkeys we are now eating. Let us all give thanks."

And that was the first Thanksgiving!

Sharing the Joy of Reading

Beginning readers enjoy reading books on their own. Reading a book is a worthwhile activity in and of itself for a young reader. However, a child's reading can be even more rewarding if it is shared. This sharing can enhance your child's appreciation — both of the book and of his or her own abilities.

   Now that your child has read **Squanto and the First Thanksgiving**, you can help extend your child's reading experience by encouraging him or her to:

- Retell the story or key concepts presented in this story in his or her own words. The retelling can be oral or written.

- Create a picture of a favorite character, event, or concept from this book.

- Express his or her own ideas and feelings about the subject of this book and other things he or she might want to know about this subject.

Here is an activity that you can do together to help extend your child's appreciation of this book: Help your child use small paper bags, paper and wooden sticks, or other suitable materials to make two simple stick puppets, one of Squanto, and one of a Pilgrim man or woman. Then invite your child to present a puppet show in which Squanto teaches the Pilgrim how to farm, fish, and hunt, and the Pilgrim invites Squanto to the Thanksgiving feast.